# THE GEM HUNTER'S HANDBOOK

Tim Lutz

# RUNNING PRESS
PHILADELPHIA • LONDON

Copyright © 1990 by Running Press
Printed in Canada. All rights reserved under the Pan-American and International Copyright Conventions.

Canadian representatives: General Publishing Co., Ltd., 30 Lesmill Road, Don Mills, Ontario M3B 2T6.

12

Digit on the right indicates the number of this printing.

Library of Congress Cataloging-in-Publication Number 90–53335
ISBN 0–89471–828–2

Gemological consultant: John Skidmore
Editor: Steven Zorn
Picture researcher: Gillian Speeth
Book interior design by Robert Perry
Package and book cover design by Toby Schmidt
Package front and back illustrations by Bob Walters
Package back photographs: (top) The Bettmann Archive; (bottom) Courtesy the Australian Overseas Information Service.
Package photographs by Bel-Hop Studios
Book cover photographs: Top row, left to right: 1. Sapphire, 2. Labradorite (Feldspar), 3. Kunzite. Second row: 4. Opal, 5. Emerald, 6. Opal. Third row: 7. Citrine, 8. Amethyst. Fourth row: 9. Opal, 10. Aquamarine, 11. Turquoise. Fifth row: 12. Amethyst, 13. Opal, 14. Sapphire.
Book cover photo sources: Gemological Institute of America: 1, 5, and 12 © 1989; 3, 8, and 10 © 1989/R. Weldon; 7 © 1989/Mike Havstad; 14 © 1989/Tino Hammid. Courtesy the American Museum of Natural History, Department of Library Services: 2, 11. Aldo Tutino/Art Resources/New York: 4, 6, and 9. Courtesy the Australian Overseas Information Service: 13.
Book interior photographs: Alinari/Art Resource, New York: pp. 14, 23 (top). Courtesy the American Museum of Natural History, Department of Library Services. p. 32 (left) neg. no. 2A9042 (Photo by Rota); (right) neg. no. 121800 (Photo by Thane Bierwert); p. 50, neg. no 2923B; p. 51, (no 2), neg. no 41971; (no. 4), neg. no. R-132-5; (no. 5), neg. no. 12047; (no. 7), neg. no. 38182; (no. 8), neg. no. 2A2414 (Photo by L. Bottin); (no. 9), neg. no 298138 (Photo by Edward R. Bailey). Art Resource, New York: p. 25 (left). Courtesy the Australian Overseas Information Service: p. 38. The Bettmann Archive: pp. 7, 8, 21, 35, 36. Courtesy British Information Services: p. 30 (top). Courtesy the British Tourist Authority: page 11. Courtesy the Diamond Information Center: p. 62. Giraudon/Art Resource, New York: pp. 13, 25 (right). Courtesy Japan Airlines: p. 17 (top and bottom). Courtesy Japan National Tourist Organization: p. 18. Courtesy Netherlands Board of Tourism: p. 12. Photo Researchers, Inc.: p. 49, © Carl Frank 1972; p. 47, © Barry Lopez 1974; p. 20, © Tom McHugh 19732. Reuters/Bettmann Newsphotos: pp. 30 (bottom), 42. Smithsonian Institution: p. 39, neg. no. 788853A. Courtesy the U.S. Geological Survey/W.T. Schaller: p. 51 (nos. 3 and 6). Courtesy The United Nations: pp. 23 (bottom), 24, 28, 37, 52. Courtesy The United Nations/Photo by Alon Reininger: pp. 10, 51 (no. 10). The University Museum, University of Pennsylvania: p. 26, neg. no. 139420. UPS/Bettmann Newsphotos: pp. 27, 29.
Book interior illustrations by Christine Coligan & Michael Morrison
Typography by Commcor Communications Corporation, Philadelphia, Pennsylvania

This book may be ordered by mail from the publisher. Please add $2.50 for postage and handling. *But try your bookstore first!*

Running Press Book Publishers
125 South Twenty-second Street
Philadelphia, Pennsylvania 19103–4399

**About the Author**
**Tim Lutz** is a geologist who specializes in the study of igneous rocks. He teaches geology at LaSalle University and West Chester University, in the Philadelphia area. He earned his Ph.D. in geology at the University of Pennsylvania.

# CONTENTS

# PART ONE

# What Are Gems?

**W**e read about gems in books and see them in movies. In stories they're found in jungles by brave explorers or in hotel safes by clever thieves. Sometimes they cover the robes of kings and queens or fill the treasure chests of dangerous pirates. They're bought by the wealthy for large sums of money or found in tunnels by laboring miners. Gems always seem to be where the action is!

The question, "What is a gem?," doesn't have a short answer because many things can be gems. Most gems are minerals found in the ground, but some, like pearls and ivory, are made by animals. Even fossilized tree sap, called amber, can be a gem.

The value of gems is based on four factors: beauty, durability, rarity, and fashion. Not all gems rate well in all four ways. For example, turquoise is beautiful and fashionable but not especially rare or durable, while garnet is beautiful and durable but not very rare or fashionable.

You may be wondering what a mineral is. Minerals, like everything else, are made of atoms. In minerals, the atoms form an orderly arrangement and produce crystal shapes. Liquids and gases can't be minerals because the atoms are free to move around. But not all solids are minerals, either. For example, glass is a solid in which the atoms are scrambled, even though glass looks and feels smooth.

A single mineral can form several varieties of gems, depending on what impurities are present. For example, the mineral corundum, usually brown, may become the red gem we call a ruby when just a tiny bit of the element chromium is added. Blue sapphires are also made of corundum.

Captain Kidd, the notorious pirate, buries his hoard of stolen gems.

A Navaho woman proudly displays her turquoise jewelry.

# PROPERTIES OF GEM MINERALS

Have you ever noticed that a spoon in a glass of water looks bent when viewed from the side? That's because light rays bend or change direction as they go from air to water.

Light entering a transparent (clear) crystal also bends. Some crystals bend light more than others, and the further the light is bent, the more light is reflected back to you, and the more sparkling or brilliant the gem appears. If someone you know has a diamond ring, compare the brilliance of the diamond with a piece of ice. The diamond bends light almost twice as far as ice, making it much more brilliant.

Besides brilliance, another quality of transparent gems is their ability to act like prisms and to break light into colors. The sparkling flashes of color given off by diamond comes from this property, called dispersion. The higher a mineral's dispersion, the better prism it is.

The most dazzling gem in the world wouldn't be worth

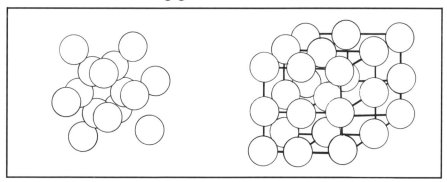

When carbon atoms are disorganized (left), they form soft, black graphite. When they're orderly, the result is diamond.

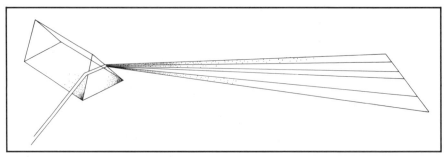

As light passes through a prism, it's broken into rainbow colors.

much if it scratched easily. Hardness, or durability, is an important property of gems. Each mineral has a hardness that can be measured. This property is a clue to identifying the mineral. You'll learn more about this on page 49.

The value of most gems depends on the lack of flaws such as cracks, bubbles, or pieces of other minerals (called inclusions) that mar their beauty. For example, diamonds are graded based on the absence of flaws, a quality called clarity. On the other hand, some minerals are made more valuable by inclusions. The gem aventurine is a type of quartz that contains tiny inclusions of other minerals that give the gem a striking green or red color. Star sapphires contain inclusions that reflect light in the form of a six-rayed star. Opal is a beautiful gem in which very small spheres of mineral material are surrounded by water. Light entering gem opal is broken into flashes of color so unusual that the effect, called opalescence (O-puh-LES-ents), is named after the gem.

One day's production of diamonds from a single mine.

# GEMS BY THE POUND?

After color and clarity, size is the next most important factor in determining a gem's value. Gemstones used in jewelry are measured by their weight in carats. A carat is a very small weight—a single penny weighs around 15 carats. Most diamonds used in engagement rings weigh between 1/4 carat and two carats. A diamond or ruby weighing as much as a penny would be very unusual in a ring.

The world's largest diamond, called the Cullinan, was discovered in South Africa in 1905. It weighed 3,106 carats (about 1⅓ pounds, or 207 pennies!). Crystals of other gems can get much bigger. Several crystals of topaz found in Brazil weighed more than 500 pounds each. Such huge stones aren't measured in carats. If they were, they'd weigh much more than a million carats apiece.

A gem to be used in jewelry is usually cut either into a cabochon (KAB-uh-shon) shape, with a smooth, domed top, or into a shape with a number of flat surfaces, called facets. The cabochon is usually used for gems that are opaque, such as agate or turquoise. Cabochons also show off the star in star sapphire better than a facet cut. Transparent gems, such as diamonds, rubies, and sapphires, are most often cut with facets that allow light to enter and exit the stone from many angles, showing off the stone's brilliance and fire.

A royal treasure from the British Crown Jewels.

Some traditional facet cuts (from left): the brilliant cut, the emerald cut, the marquise cut, and the pear shape.

Gem cutting is a delicate and tricky procedure. A gem cutter, also known as a lapidary, has to plan to remove any parts of a stone that contain flaws or inclusions, while keeping as much of the stone as possible. Sometimes, in order to turn a rough stone into a flawless gem, up to half of the stone's weight may be lost. A large stone may also be cut into a number of pieces.

The Cullinan diamond was cut into 105 gems. The largest, called the Star of Africa, weighs 530 carats (as much as 35 pennies) and is now in the Royal Sceptre of the British Crown Jewels. If cut into a sphere, this gem would be 1½ inches across. Eight of the other gems were unusually large, and 96 were of ordinary size (weighing a few carats or less). Amazingly, the Cullinan was sent to England from South Africa by regular mail rather than by messenger when it was to be cut, probably to avoid the attention of thieves.

Perhaps you already know that diamond is the hardest material on earth, but

Grinding diamond facets

did you ever wonder how it's possible to cut a diamond? The answer is that there are certain directions in a diamond, determined by the arrangement of its atoms, along which it can be split. Specially-designed steel tools and paper-thin saw blades coated with diamond dust are used to cut large stones into smaller, flawless ones. Flat facets are made by grinding and polishing the stone with diamond dust. All other minerals are much less hard than diamond and can easily be cut and polished using diamond tools.

# GETTING RARER

For most of human history, mineral gems have been difficult to obtain, and this has added to their value. Europeans in the Middle Ages could get sapphires and diamonds only from India. For a European to hunt these gems meant a long,

Medieval relic case

dangerous journey. Traders coming to Europe from the East could sell gems at high prices. Even in India it was difficult to find diamonds and rubies. Today we know that even in the richest diamond mines, the chances that a pebble contains a diamond is only about one in eight million, and only one out of every four diamonds is likely to be of gem quality.

Most minerals occur both in ordinary and in more rare

This sixth-century mosaic shows the Roman empress Theodora in her jewels.

gem forms. The mineral quartz, in tiny white crystals, rounded by the waves, is a common ingredient of beach sand. Quartz in this form is not considered a gem—anyone could collect tons of it! The more rare, large crystals of quartz with flat faces are much more valuable, as are crystals with color. The gem amethyst is purple quartz, and citrine is yellow quartz. You can think of amethyst and citrine as two different members of the quartz ''family''—a group of gem minerals that also includes rose (pink) quartz and smoky (gray) quartz.

Natural gems are becoming more rare all the time because they can take millions of years to form. The gems that are being mined today were formed long ago, and new gems

are not forming nearly fast enough to replace them. In this way, mineral gems are non-renewable resources like the oil, coal, and uranium that we use for energy.

# GEMS FROM THE LAB

For centuries, people have looked for substitutes for gems. For example, cut glass has been used to simulate diamond. These glass "diamonds" are much less rare and less expensive than the real thing, but they are also less beautiful and durable.

Since 1900, scientists have manufactured forms of minerals, called mineraloids, in the lab. Gem-quality mineraloids are called synthetic gems.

To manufacture gems in a lab, scientists usually must recreate the conditions under which the gem is formed in nature. Since synthetic gems are made from the same minerals as natural gems, they have exactly the same properties as natural gems, and are often just as beautiful. Even a gem expert, called a gemologist, might find it difficult or impossible to tell the difference. The value of some natural stones has been decreased by the marketing of synthetic gems.

Diamond is a mineral that forms under the extreme pressures and temperatures that exist more than 100 miles beneath the earth's surface. The first synthetic diamonds were made in 1955 by putting carbon under pressures of more than 600,000 pounds per square inch at temperatures of more than 1,400° F.

Carbon is one of the most plentiful elements on earth. Coal and the black soot left by a smoking candle are mostly

carbon. It turns out that the source of the carbon is not important in making diamonds—even carbon from burnt peanut butter has been used. Today, tens of tons of synthetic diamonds are produced each year.

If so many diamonds are being manufactured, why are they still much more expensive than a big jar of peanut butter? Although we can make diamonds, it's very difficult to duplicate the effects of the millions of years during which natural diamonds form. Synthetic diamonds are tiny crystals suitable for industrial purposes, but not for gems. It's possible to make gem diamonds in the lab—but only under conditions that make them more expensive than natural diamonds. New techniques in Japan and elsewhere are lowering the cost of producing gem-quality synthetic diamonds.

Scientists can synthesize gems that aren't found in nature. Among the most popular of these is cubic zirconia, first synthesized in 1976. Cubic zirconia has a brilliance and dispersion similar to those of diamond, although cubic zirconia is not as hard. Cubic zirconia forms at such high temperatures (around 5,000° F) that it took scientists years to develop a container to hold it while it was being synthesized. Now special water-cooled containers are used. Other synthetic gems are used in lasers and other electronic devices.

# GEMS THAT AREN'T MINERALS

Earlier, we mentioned some gems that aren't minerals. Among these are pearl, coral, ivory, amber, and jet. All of these gem materials, except amber and jet, are made by animals. Amber and jet are produced by plants. These non-

minerals may possess the same qualities as mineral gems: beauty, durability, rarity, and fashion.

# Pearls

Ocean-dwelling shellfish, especially oysters, make pearls when they are irritated by a grain of sand inside their shell! If the sand can't be removed, the animal covers it with a substance it makes, called nacre. The shellfish coats the sand with layer upon layer of nacre, building the pearl slowly over a period of years.

Like mineral gems, pearls form in a variety of colors, including white, rose, yellow, blue, green, and dark gray (sometimes called black pearls). Pearls can be any shape, from round as marbles to really weird shapes, called baroque pearls. The most fashionable gem pearls are round and are white, rose, or black. Fewer than 1 in 10,000

A perfect pearl is harvested from an oyster.

Sorting pearls by size and color

In Japan, pearl diving is done by women. It's dangerous, difficult work.

oysters contain gem pearls. The largest pearl was discovered in a shellfish called an abalone. The pearl weighed more than 14 pounds! If this pearl were round, it would be 6½ inches across.

Pearls are not as durable as most mineral gems, and they must be handled carefully to prevent wear.

Hundreds of years ago, the Chinese discovered that irritants could be added to oysters to make them grow pearls. This process was developed further by the Japanese, who put tiny spheres made of the shell linings of oysters (called mother-of-pearl) into other oysters. The "seeded" oysters are kept on trays hung below rafts so they can be collected easily.

During a period of about one to six years, the oysters deposit nacre on the seed sphere, just as they would on a sand grain. The pearls that are formed in this way are called cultured pearls. Cultured pearls are nearly identical to natural pearls and there is no great difference in price between them.

According to legend, the Egyptian queen Cleopatra made a bet with Roman ruler Mark Antony that she could eat the most expensive meal. She won the bet by dissolving a pearl earring in a bowl of vinegar and drinking it.

Coral is most valuable as shelter for many species of sea life.

# Coral

Coral is a gem made by small, soft-bodied creatures called polyps that live in colonies on the ocean floor. To protect themselves, they form a "skeleton" of a mineral deposit. After the animals die, the coral is left behind. The Great Barrier Reef of Australia, which is more than 1,250 miles long, is made of coral that has built up over millions of years. Coral communities are very delicate, and in some places they are endangered.

The precious coral that is valued as a gem comes from the Mediterranean Sea and the Sea of Japan. When polished,

this coral is red, rose, or pink, and it is often used to make beads.

An unusual type of gem is fossilized coral. Coral that formed more than 350 million years ago is found as water-rounded pebbles near Petoskey, Michigan. The smooth surfaces of these pebbles show off the intricate structure of the coral, although they are not brightly colored like precious coral. ''Petoskey stones'' are the state stone of Michigan.

# Ivory

Ivory is the material that forms elephant tusks and the teeth of certain animals, including hippopotamuses and whales. It is creamy white or pink and is durable, though it can be carved easily enough to be used in jewelry.

The animals from which ivory is obtained are now endangered by extinction, and ivory hunting and importing is outlawed in most countries. This is one case where the rarity of a gem may make it undesirable.

Most ivory has come from elephant tusks. However, in

In the eighteenth century, sailors carved scrimshaw from whale teeth.

the 1700s and 1800s, American sailors on whaling ships made distinctive carvings, called scrimshaw, from the teeth of sperm whales.

# Amber

Amber is an unusual gem because it's actually a fossil, often millions of years old. This dull, yellow gem forms when sap oozes from a pine tree. The sap may collect on the tree in a blob that falls when it dries. Over many, many years, the blob of sap hardens into amber. If you keep your eyes open when you take a walk in the woods, you may see droplets of sap—future amber—on a tree.

We know that amber is very old because it sometimes contains extinct insects or plants. In fact, amber is more valuable if it does contain an insect. The oldest known amber formed more than 300 million years ago.

# Jet

Like amber, jet is also a fossil. It's a rare form of coal prized for its velvety-black color, from which the expression "jet black" comes. Jet is durable and is easily carved.

Although it has been used since Roman times, jet reached the height of its popularity in England in the 1800s, when it was worn at funerals. The largest jet deposits were in northeast England. Today, jet is out of fashion. The need for black jewelry and buttons has been taken over almost entirely by plastics.

People of all cultures wear jewels. The top picture shows King Henry VIII of England. Below him is a young girl from Nepal.

# GEMS AND HISTORY

Gems have fascinated people since the beginning of history. Myths and folktales show that gems were important good luck charms and religious symbols for ancient people. Some gems were thought to have the power to heal or to give magic powers to those who possessed them. And gems have also been worn for thousands of years simply as ornaments in jewelry, much as we wear them today.

At first, gems were commonly used in their natural state because their hardness made them difficult to cut. However, engraved gems were made 6,000 years ago in Mesopotamia, a kingdom in what is now the country of Iraq. These gems were carved with symbols that identified their owners. They were used to make impressions on the wax that sealed documents. Those

who received the documents could be sure of who sent them and that the contents had not been revealed.

Imagine. . .more than 2,300 years ago, in Persia, a crowd gathers to pay its respects at the funeral of a noblewoman whose body lies in a bronze casket. The mourners hold jewelry of amazing beauty and value.

As the time for burial comes, an astonishing thing happens: the people drop their jewels and charms into the casket, believing that the gems will keep the woman safe and comfortable in her afterlife.

The woman and her jewels remained secure until archeologists discovered the casket buried deep in the earth. From finds such as these, we know that gems were a more vital part of life than they are today.

Imagine. . .more than 1,600 years ago, a ship is preparing to sail from Greece. To protect them from the dangers of the journey, the crew take with them seven charms set with gems. Coral is attached to the front of the ship to save it from the winds and waves. Other gems are believed to protect the sailors from drowning, from evil spells,

A Chinese performer

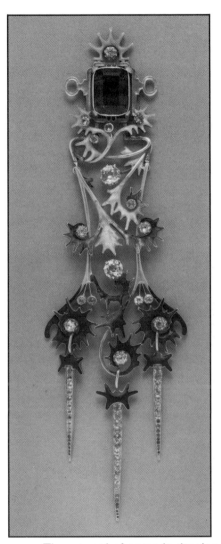

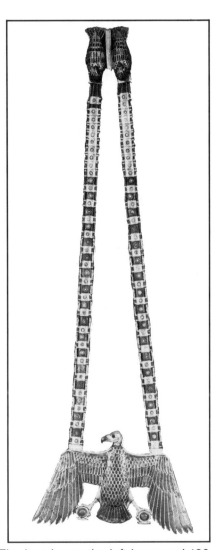

The appeal of gems is timeless. The jewelry on the left is around 100 years old; the piece on the right is more than 3,000 years old.

and from storms. Without these charms the sailors would not leave shore for the dangers of the sea.

Belief in the magical powers of some gems persisted in Europe through the Middle Ages. Among the last gem "magic" to disappear was the practice of gazing into rock crystal balls to tell the future or to see distant places. There is no scientific support for the belief that crystal balls contain any power to reveal the future.

Most people today don't believe that gems are necessary for safe sailing or a comfortable afterlife. However, our custom

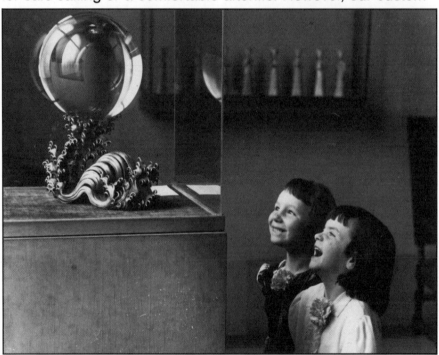

These girls are looking at their reflections—not their futures—in this pure rock crystal ball.

of wearing birthstones goes back to ancient ideas about how the magic in gems came from the stars and planets.

The fame that some gems have today is a sign of the status they once held as jewels that could only be obtained by the very wealthy or the very powerful. Some of these gems have long histories of ownership which, given their value, sometimes include murder and theft.

Some of the most famous gems are now turning up in museums. The Hope Diamond had a long and colorful history before arriving at the Smithsonian Institution in Washington,

A chic London model uses gems to make a fashion statement.

This Panamanian woman adorns her hair with pearls and precious metals.

Virtuoso pianist Liberace dazzled audiences with his wardrobe and jewelry.

D.C. The Hope is a blue diamond of 112 carats that was probably discovered in India. It was brought to Europe around 1668 and sold it to the French king, Louis XIV, who had it cut into a 67-carat stone. It was stolen from the French Crown Jewels in 1792, and it reappeared in London, having been cut into a stone of 45 carats to help disguise it.

It had a succession of owners, including, in 1830, banker Thomas Hope, from whom it acquired its present name. One owner, a Washington socialite, treated the diamond like a toy, letting her dog wear it and allowing her guests to play catch with it!

Some people began to believe the Hope Diamond was cursed when several of its owners suffered financial or personal disasters. Finally, the jewel was acquired by a gem

Her Majesty Queen Elizabeth II of England (top) and Princess Diana wear exquisite tiaras befitting their noble positions.

dealer who donated it to the Smithsonian in 1958. A few people still believe in the Hope curse, and tend to blame the stone for every national disaster.

# WHAT GEM HUNTERS MUST KNOW

Now that you know what gems are, it's time to consider how and where they are formed, because this is important information for a gem hunter.

Minerals don't occur mixed up with one another in unpredictable ways. Certain conditions have to exist for a particular mineral, like quartz, to form. Minerals that form under the same conditions as quartz are likely to be found with quartz. Granite is a common rock because the conditions required for its main minerals, quartz and feldspar, to form occur frequently. If we're looking for a variety of feldspar, like green amazonite, we'd look first for granite.

The gem topaz is also usually associated with granites, and it's often found along with quartz in veins near granite.

Some of the rules for finding gems involve knowing what common minerals a gem is *not* associated with. For example, corundum *never* forms in rocks with quartz. So a granite would be a bad place to look for rubies or sapphires, the gem forms of corundum.

The study of how and why rocks form is called petrology, which is a branch of geology, the study of the earth. Most gem minerals form in rocks deep within the earth under conditions of extremely high temperature and pressure. When these rocks are exposed on the earth's surface, some minerals break down

into clay and other particles, called sediments. The more durable minerals, including the gems, do not break down but are carried away in streams.

Some sediments are carried out to sea by rivers, and accumulate deep in the oceans. The grains of quartz sand on a beach may originally have formed in a granite, but only the quartz sediment remains because it's more durable than feldspar. Over time, the quartz sand could turn into a sedimentary rock, called sandstone.

Gem minerals are usually mined from sediments and sedimentary rocks, not the rocks in which they originally formed. Many gem minerals have a property, known as density, that prevents them from being carried far in flowing water and improves our chances of finding them on land. Dense materials are heavy for their size.

You can understand density and imagine what happens in a stream by blowing gently on a mixture of sand and pepper. The pepper will be blown away easily, while the more dense sand tends to remain behind. In flowing streams, the most dense materials settle out first, along with larger pieces of less dense minerals, and form deposits called placers. Gem

Crystals of garnet

A vein of turquoise

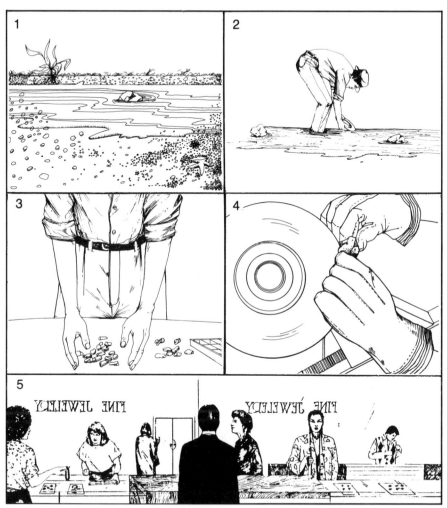

Gem minerals form underground. Some wash into a stream with other sediments (fig. 1). A gem hunter pans through sediments to find gems (fig. 2). The gem minerals are sorted (fig. 3). The best ones are cut and polished (fig. 4). The finished gems are mounted and sold (fig. 5).

placers usually form deposits called gravels that are much coarser than sand. Placer gravels are the major sources of diamonds, rubies, sapphires, and emeralds found today.

Several types of scientists and other professionals are involved in hunting gems. Geologists are scientists who study all aspects of the earth, and mineralogists are geologists who specialize in minerals. Gemologists are specialists in gem minerals and other gems, such as pearls and amber. They determine the quality of gems at every stage, from sorting gems for a mining company, to selling them in a jewelry shop.

# MINING GEMS

Despite what we know about how gems form and where to find them, some of the most famous gem finds have been made by accident.

In 1867, a farmer in South Africa noticed his children playing with an unusual pebble, about 1/2 inch across, they had found on a river bank. When the farmer took the pebble to the city, it was identified as a 22-carat diamond. A second diamond was found in the same area by a shepherd in 1869. By 1870 the news had spread over the world and many people came to South Africa to try to make their fortunes by diamond mining. South Africa is still a leading producer of diamonds.

The first South African diamond hunters "panned" for diamonds in placer deposits. In panning, sediment is put in a shallow pan similar to a large pie dish or a Chinese wok, and the sediment is swirled with water so that the lighter minerals are carried away and the dense diamonds are left behind. This method works with any dense material and was used by gold

miners during the California gold rush in the 1850s, an event similar to the African "diamond rush."

By looking at the places where diamonds were found in rivers, it was possible to trace the diamonds to their source rocks, and these were mined, too.

To mine gems from rock, the rock is broken into pieces small enough to free the gems from the rock. This is a delicate

Digging diamonds in South Africa, 1872

job because very large gems have a chance of being destroyed. A diamond of about 1,500 carats was seen in the same mine that yielded the Cullinan diamond, but was crushed by heavy equipment before it could be removed. It was thought that this diamond and the Cullinan might

Working in cramped underground conditions, miners prepare to blast diamond-bearing ore from the surrounding rock.

Diamonds in the rough

have once been part of a single stone that would have weighed almost 5,000 carats and been more than 3 inches across!

The fate of the crushed diamond shows that even extremely durable gems can be damaged if they are not treated properly.

To separate the gems from the other minerals around them, the crushed rock is put in liquids that are heavier (more dense) than the unwanted minerals, but lighter than the gems. The gems sink and the other minerals float away.

Most gems are mined by huge companies, but opal mines in Australia are limited in size by law. These mines are operated by families or a few partners. The land is parceled into claims, each run by a single group, that are exploited by

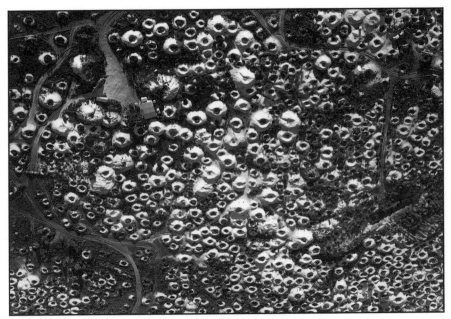

The many opal mines of Australia look like ant hills when viewed from the air.

digging small pits or tunnels. Because explosives are used underground to break the rock, the work is dangerous.

Not all gems are found in such far-away places as Africa and Australia. The United States is rich in gem localities, and almost every state has some history of gem mining. For example, North Carolina has deposits of emerald, ruby, and moonstone. Nevada has opal and turquoise. Diamonds have been found in sediments in several areas of the United States, including the Appalachian Mountains from Virginia to Georgia, the Great Lakes region, and California. Diamonds in their source rock have been found at Murfreesboro, Arkansas, where the largest U.S. diamond (40 carats) was found in 1924.

The Hope Diamond has a long and colorful history.

In some places old mines are now parks or are owned by companies that permit gem collecting for a fee. You can pay to look for diamonds in Murfreesboro's Craters of Diamonds State Park. In Herkimer, New York, you can hunt excellent crystals of quartz for a fee. Sapphire mining in sediments has been opened to the public in Montana.

# PART TWO

# Buried
# Treasures

**G**em minerals are sold and traded by museums and individuals, as well as by gem merchants and jewelers. It is as an individual, or as part of a school or museum expedition, that you're likely to gain experience as a gem hunter. Doing your own gem hunting involves several activities. First there's field work, the process of going outdoors to find gem minerals. Then you'll identify and catalog your finds. Finally, you may want to display your minerals or fashion the best gems into jewelry.

Prospectors sift through gravel in search of diamonds in South Africa.

# FIELD WORK

The important part of field work is planning and preparation. Reference materials are used to find where rocks with interesting minerals are found. Maps can help you locate your finds. You can find gem-collecting books in your school or public library. Some books list places to collect specific gems, and local mineral collecting clubs and rock shops may have information, too. Mineral clubs will also help you find people to go into the field with you.

Whether you're going out for an afternoon on the beach or a week in the mountains, there are some things you will want to take along. A sturdy notebook to keep a record of your hunt is the most important. A small field pack is useful for carrying your equipment and for bringing back your samples. Collecting containers, masking tape, pens, and markers should be in your pack, along with the tools that you'll use to identify minerals in the field. Wherever you go, wear protective footwear and clothing.

People who look for gems in rocks sometimes use rock hammers or chisels to help them break the rocks apart. If you do this, first get instructions for using your equipment, and always wear heavy gloves and safety glasses to protect yourself. A small first-aid kit with bandages and antiseptic may come in handy, too. Before you go off to explore, be sure to tell someone where you're going and when you expect to be back.

When you go in the field to have fun collecting, respect the rights and privacy of others. Many public parks have regulations that prohibit collecting so that the rocks and minerals will always be there for everyone to see. Check the regulations before you go, and if necessary, ask for permission

at the park office. If you can't collect, you can still learn about minerals by looking.

If you want to go on private property, ask the owner for permission. Most of the time the owner will be happy to let you look, and will be pleased that you asked.

Gems and gemlike minerals can be found in many field environments: stream beds or banks, beaches, soil, or in rocks. Keep careful notes on what you see and where you see it. Remember that each type of mineral forms under its own particular conditions. By studying and identifying the rocks and sediments in an area, you can make a good guess about the kind of gem minerals you're likely to find there. If you find one gem, there might be more nearby, and others might be found in areas with similar kinds of rocks.

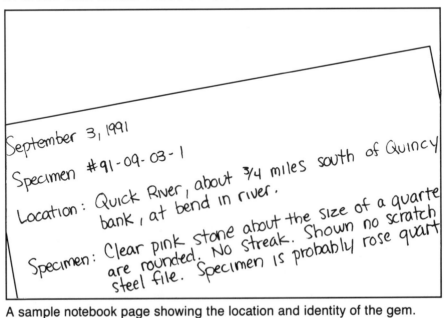

September 3, 1991

Specimen #91-09-03-1

Location: Quick River, about 3/4 miles south of Quincy bank, at bend in river.

Specimen: Clear pink stone about the size of a quarter are rounded. No streak. Shown no scratch steel file. Specimen is probably rose quart

A sample notebook page showing the location and identity of the gem.

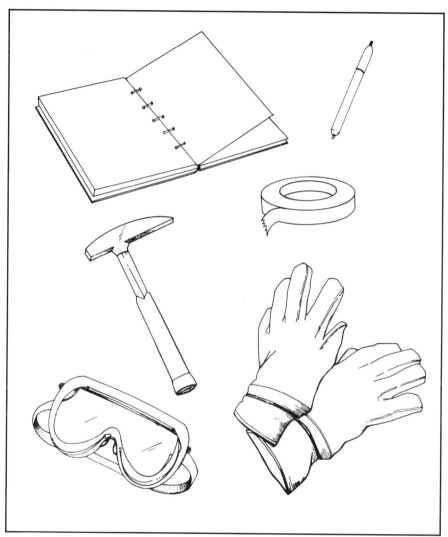

Basic gem hunter's supplies include a notebook, pens and markers, masking tape, a geological hammer, work gloves, and safety goggles.

Reviewing your notes will help you see patterns in where you find gems. For example, you might discover that in streams, gems are found mostly in the sediment where the stream bends. This could occur because the water slows down at bends, allowing the denser minerals to settle out while the others are washed past. Your notes will also keep you from going back to places where you didn't find anything.

# KEEPING TRACK

Every sample you collect should be labeled with a number that tells when you found it. This number is called a field number. The first mineral you collect on the 3rd of September, 1991 could be labeled "91–09–03–1," the second mineral, "91–09–03–2," and so on. The labels can be written on small pieces of masking tape stuck to the sample. Or you can put a dab of white paint on the specimen and write the number on it when it dries.

Minerals in a specimen tray

You can keep small or easily broken specimens in tiny, labeled boxes or empty film canisters. Be sure the minerals from different boxes don't get mixed up.

In your notebook, write the number of the specimen, its description, and when and where you found it. Later, as you examine and identify the specimens at home, you can add new information, such as how you identified the mineral.

Iris agate

# SORTING THEM OUT

To identify minerals accurately in the laboratory, mineralogists use scientific techniques that involve shining a beam of light through slices of a mineral only 1/1000 of an inch thick, and bouncing X rays off layers of atoms in a crystal that are less than 1/10,000,000 of an inch apart. These methods give extremely detailed information about a mineral's crystal structure and chemical composition, which makes it easy to identify the minerals.

In the field, less sophisticated methods are needed. You'll learn how to identify minerals by studying their physical properties, such as color, hardness, and density.

**Color** is the easiest property to see, but don't rely only on a mineral's color to identify it. Many gems are the same color. Emerald, alexandrite, and actinolite are all green gems. Still, color is an important property, so you should record color in your field notes.

Try to judge the color of your samples using the same light source and background for each one. You can compare the colors of your minerals to the names of colors in a set of colored pencils or crayons. Scientists call such references color standards. You can decide whether a mineral looks more like red, vermillion, or scarlet.

If your specimen doesn't look like any colors in your set, imagine what mixture of colors it looks like. You can even draw a patch of color in your notebook to show the color of the mineral.

**Streak** is a special color property of minerals. To determine a mineral's streak, you need a streak plate, which you can buy at a mineral shop. Or you can go to a plumbing supply store and ask for a piece of ceramic tile. The white, unglazed side of the tile is as good as a streak plate.

Rub the mineral on the plate and see if a colored streak is left behind. The color of the streak isn't always the same color as the mineral. If there is no color, the mineral is said to have no streak. Some minerals are harder than the streak plate, and will leave no streak.

**Luster** refers to the surface appearance of a mineral, but not to its color. For example, a piece of glass, a book cover, a shirt, and a rug can all be red, but each has a different appearance, ranging from very shiny to very rough and dull.

Minerals have a *metallic* luster if they look like a new coin. Minerals that are glassy-looking are said to have a

*vitreous* luster, while those that appear as hard and brilliant as diamond are said to be *adamantine.* A *pearly* luster is named after the deep, glimmering glow of pearls. *Dull* luster can be seen on a streak plate. A mineral with a *waxy* luster looks like a lump of wax.

**Hardness** is measured by finding out whether one material can scratch, or be scratched by, another. Mineralogists use mineral standards that are numbered on a scale from 1 (the softest) to 10 (the hardest). This scale, called the Mohs scale, is shown in Table 1. If a mineral has a hardness of 3, a mineralogist writes it as "H=3." Your kit contains two minerals on the Mohs scale: fluorite (H=4) and amazonite (H=6).

Naturally formed emerald crystals

In the field, you don't have to carry the minerals on the Mohs scale because you can bring along some convenient substitutes. Your fingernail has a hardness of about 2. A penny has a hardness of about 3. If a mineral scratches your fingernail but not a penny, it has a hardness between 2 and 3. For harder minerals, you'll need a tool of steel. A pocket knife usually has H=5–5.5, a hardened steel file, H=6.5.

Sometimes minerals develop weathered surfaces that are softer than the rest of the mineral. Test the hardness using the freshest surface or edge you can find. When trying to make a scratch, be careful not to press so hard that the mineral breaks—it could be a gem! Be sure to wear your safety glasses to protect your eyes, and make sure you learn how to use tools, such as a knife or file, before you begin.

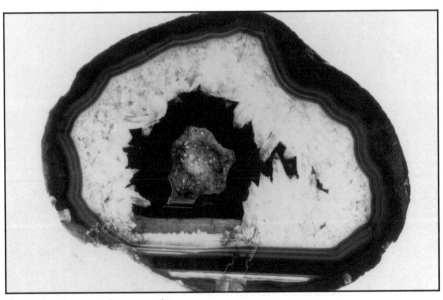

Crystals of quartz in a geode

## Table 1

| The Mohs Scale | | |
| --- | --- | --- |
| | Hardness | Mineral |
| | 1 | Talc |
| | 2 | Gypsum |
| | 3 | Calcite |
| | 4 | Fluorite |
| | 5 | Apatite |
| | 6 | Feldspar (Amazonite, Moonstone) |
| | 7 | Quartz (Amethyst, Citrine) |
| | 8 | Topaz |
| | 9 | Corundum (Ruby, Sapphire) |
| | 10 | Diamond |

**Density** is how heavy something is for its size. For example, a lump of hematite, which contains a lot of iron, will be more dense than a lump of quartz of equal size.

To identify a mineral, it'll help you to have a list of the characteristic properties of several minerals. Table 2 shows the properties of various gem minerals. You can compare a mineral you've found to those in the table. If you're lucky, only one mineral in the table will match, and you will have made an identification!

Don't be discouraged if you can't positively identify all your minerals. Even expert mineralogists can't identify every mineral they find without using more sophisticated tests.

If a diamond's facets aren't precise, the diamond won't sparkle.

Follow the instructions on pages 48–51 to determine an unknown mineral's luster and hardness. Compare your findings with the properties listed in Table 2. The left-hand column tells you the name of the gem. The right-hand column tells you what family the gem or mineral belongs to.

For example, if you're lucky enough to find a blue stone with a hardness of 9 and a vitreous luster, you may have found a sapphire, which is a form of the mineral corundum.

Table 2

| Mineral Properties | | | | |
|---|---|---|---|---|
| Gem or Mineral | Luster | Hard-ness | Common Colors | Gem Family Name and Other Remarks |
| **Actinolite** | Vitreous | 5–6 | Green | A mineral family including some forms of jade. |
| **Agate** | Waxy | 7 | Various | Banded *chalcedony* |
| **Alexandrite** | Vitreous | 8.5 | Emerald green | Gem *chrysoberyl* |
| **Amazonite** | Vitreous | 6 | Green | Gem *feldspar* |
| **Amethyst** | Vitreous | 7 | Purple | Gem *quartz* |
| **Aquamarine** | Vitreous | 7.5–8 | Greenish-blue | Gem *beryl* |
| **Aventurine** | Vitreous | 7 | Red or green | Gem *quartz* (with inclusions) |
| **Carnelian** | Waxy | 7 | Red | *Chalcedony* |
| **Citrine** | Vitreous | 7 | Yellow | Gem *quartz* |

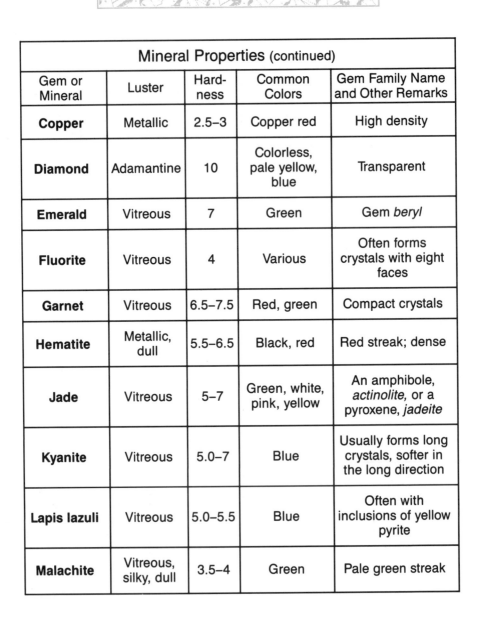

| Mineral Properties (continued) | | | | |
|---|---|---|---|---|
| Gem or Mineral | Luster | Hard-ness | Common Colors | Gem Family Name and Other Remarks |
| **Copper** | Metallic | 2.5–3 | Copper red | High density |
| **Diamond** | Adamantine | 10 | Colorless, pale yellow, blue | Transparent |
| **Emerald** | Vitreous | 7 | Green | Gem *beryl* |
| **Fluorite** | Vitreous | 4 | Various | Often forms crystals with eight faces |
| **Garnet** | Vitreous | 6.5–7.5 | Red, green | Compact crystals |
| **Hematite** | Metallic, dull | 5.5–6.5 | Black, red | Red streak; dense |
| **Jade** | Vitreous | 5–7 | Green, white, pink, yellow | An amphibole, *actinolite,* or a pyroxene, *jadeite* |
| **Kyanite** | Vitreous | 5.0–7 | Blue | Usually forms long crystals, softer in the long direction |
| **Lapis lazuli** | Vitreous | 5.0–5.5 | Blue | Often with inclusions of yellow pyrite |
| **Malachite** | Vitreous, silky, dull | 3.5–4 | Green | Pale green streak |

| Mineral Properties (continued) | | | | |
|---|---|---|---|---|
| Gem or Mineral | Luster | Hard-ness | Common Colors | Gem Family Name and Other Remarks |
| **Moonstone** | Vitreous | 6 | Blue sheen | Translucent *feldspar* |
| **Onyx** | Waxy | 7 | Various | *Chalcedony* with dark and light parallel layers |
| **Opal** | Vitreous | 6 | White, pale colors | Opalescent |
| **Quartz** | Vitreous | 7 | Various | A mineral family forming many gems |
| **Rock crystal** | Vitreous | 7 | Transparent | Gem *quartz* |
| **Ruby** | Vitreous | 9 | Red | Gem *corundum* |
| **Sapphire** | Vitreous | 9 | Blue, gray | Gem *corundum* |
| **Tourmaline** | Vitreous | 7.0–7.5 | Black, brown, green, blue, pink | Usually forms triangular, prism-shaped crystals |
| **Turquoise** | Waxy | 6 | Blue-green | Usually found in thin seams in rock |
| **Ulexite** | Silky | 2.0–2.5 | White | Usually made of many fibers |
| **Zircon** | Adamantine | 7.5 | Brown, gray, green, red | Translucent |

# MAKING A COLLECTION

After you get your minerals home you'll want to clean them and decide what to do with them. Cleaning is best done with soapy water and an old toothbrush.

Now you have to decide what to do with your specimens. Like most collectors, you'll probably find that you pick up much more in the field than you really want or have space to keep. If you meet other gem or mineral collectors, you may wish to trade some of your specimens for ones that you would like in your collection. You could list the specimens you wish to trade in one notebook, and those you want to keep in another.

Write the original sample number and a record of the specimen's provenance in your notebook. Provenance refers to a specimen's history: when and where it was found, and who collected it if you didn't. For example, a record might read: "#91–09–03–1. Rose quartz from the bank of the Quick River, just south of Quincy. Found September 3rd, 1991." If you want to find more details about this sample you could look in your field notes under #91–09–03–1.

Display your samples in open boxes or on small trays with cards that give each mineral's name and provenance. You can change your display from time to time to show off more of your collection, just as a museum does. Use themes to add interest to your displays. For example: "Gems of the Quick River," "Quartz of All Colors," or "My 10 Hardest Minerals."

When you find unusually beautiful specimens, you might want to put the gems in jewelry. Rock and hobby shops sell metal holders, cement, and other things that you can use to make necklaces, bracelets, and rings. Some gemstones can be shaped and smoothed by tumbling in a drum filled with

abrasive grit. Rock and hobby shops may sell tumbling equipment or plans so that you can build your own tumbler.

If you belong to a mineral club, the club may own a tumbler that you can use. Minerals that you find in streams or on the beach may be naturally rounded by flowing water.

Minerals and gems can be a continuing source of pleasure and recreation. For

A rock tumbler

some of us, they become a life-long hobby. For others, we make them a part of our jobs. As you continue through school, courses in earth science, geology, and geography will help you to learn more about minerals and gems.

# PART THREE

# Hunt
# Your Own
# Gems

our gem hunter's kit contains eight minerals buried in a clayey rock. Rocks like this can form from fine sediments deposited in lakes. While it's not very likely that you'll ever find such a variety of minerals in a single rock sample, it's not impossible, either.

The gem minerals that you'll be digging out of this rock are usually deposited in coarser stream sediments. But a rock like the one in your kit could have formed in a lake at the edge of a melting glacier.

Imagine a glacier moving over the country, picking up pieces of rock along the way. During its long journey, the glacier moves over many types of rocks and picks up different gems from each of them. As chunks of glacial ice break off, float away, and melt, these gems are deposited in a lake along with the fine sediments.

To begin your gem hunt, unwrap the slab and examine it. Don't worry if it's broken into pieces—this makes your job easier. You may be able to see some gems showing through the surface. If they aren't loose, don't pull them or they might break. Remember, large gems are better than small ones!

Set up your work area outdoors or in a spot indoors where a little spilled water won't hurt. If you're working indoors, cover the floor and table top with plenty of newspapers, and keep paper towels nearby to dry your hands. Fill a bucket half way with water and put it in the work area. Soak the slab in the water for at least five minutes, then pat it dry with a paper towel or piece of newspaper.

While you're soaking the slab, get your field notebook and a pen or pencil. Everything you do now is part of your gem hunt, so record things as you would in the field.

Now you're ready to find gems!

Carefully scrape away the soft clay with the wooden spatula in the kit. You could also use other tools such as a plastic knife, an old toothbrush, or toothpicks. Work slowly and carefully because most gems are durable but not indestructible. Put the slab back in water to soften it again if you need to.

As you remove the gems from the slab, dry them and attach a piece of tape to each and write a field number on it. Then write the field number and a brief description of the gem in your notebook. (You can do a detailed description later.) When you have found all eight gems, clean up your work area. Dump the bucket of dirty water outside, not down the drain.

The next step is to complete your descriptions of the gems and to identify them. Your first identifications will be a little easier than most because you already know the minerals in the kit. They are: amazonite, actinolite, copper, fluorite, hematite, kyanite, obsidian, and ulexite. You need only determine which mineral is which.

Examine the properties of each mineral—color, luster, streak, hardness, and density. Your observations, along with Table 2 on page 53 and the descriptions below, will help you identify each gem.

# WHAT YOU'VE FOUND

Here are descriptions and information about the gem minerals you've mined from the rock in this kit. Each description provides a clue to help you tell which mineral is which.

Sorting diamonds in Amsterdam.

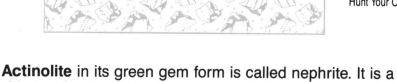

**Actinolite** in its green gem form is called nephrite. It is a form of jade. It's often found in long, needlelike crystal shapes with flat surfaces called cleavages. In the United States, nephrite has been found in Alaska and Wyoming.

**Amazonite** is the green gem form of the mineral feldspar. Crystals of amazonite are often long, and may have two flat surfaces at right angles. If you carefully examine your specimen, you'll see thin, light and dark green streaks in it. Amazonite is found in Virginia and at Pikes Peak in Colorado.

**Copper** is called a native element because it's a pure form of the element copper. Large deposits are found in northern Michigan on the Keweenaw Peninsula, and smaller deposits are known in Arizona and New Mexico.

**Fluorite** is sometimes used as a display gem because of its brilliant color. The light-colored forms, like the sample in your kit, are transparent. With a hardness of 4 on the Mohs scale, fluorite is too soft for jewelry. Deposits of fluorite are found in New Hampshire, Kentucky, Illinois, and New Mexico.

**Hematite** is named from the Greek word meaning "blood" because of the red streak it leaves on a streak plate. Large deposits of hematite are found in Michigan, Wisconsin, and Minnesota. Smaller amounts are in Alabama, Missouri, and Wyoming.

**Kyanite** is an unusual mineral because it occurs in long, blue crystals that are softer in one direction than the other. It forms at high pressures within the earth. Gem-quality kyanite has been found in Georgia and North Carolina.

**Obsidian** is natural glass formed by volcanos. It's not a mineral but a type of rock. (Remember, minerals have a regular arrangement of atoms, while glass does not.) It has a vitreous luster and a hardness of 5 to 5.5. It is usually black. It's found in many of the western states.

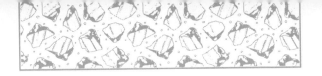

**Ulexite** is a mineral with an unusual property: when it occurs in fibers it can transmit images, earning it the nickname "television stone." Try placing your sample on top of a picture and see what happens. Ulexite is very soft (H=2 to 2.5) and can be used only for display, not in jewelry. It's found in Nevada and California.

After you have identified your minerals, you're ready to show them off. Follow the suggestions on page 56 for making your own museum displays or fashioning your own jewelry. Now you're well on your way to becoming a world-class gem-hunter!